Alikira Richard

Evaluation of WLAN Security and Performance

Wireless LAN Security

Der GRIN Verlag publiziert seit 1998 wissenschaftliche Arbeiten von Studenten, Hochschullehrern und anderen Akademikern als eBook und gedrucktes Buch. Die Verlagswebsite www.grin.com ist die ideale Plattform zur Veröffentlichung von Hausarbeiten, Abschlussarbeiten, wissenschaftlichen Aufsätzen, Dissertationen und Fachbüchern.

Document Nr. V205389

Alikira Richard

Evaluation of WLAN Security and Performance

Wireless LAN Security

GRIN Verlag

Die Deutsche Bibliothek verzeichnet diese Publikation in der Deutschen Nationalbibliografie; detaillierte bibliografische Daten sind im Internet über http://dnb.d-nb.de/ abrufbar.

1. Auflage 2012
Copyright © 2012 GRIN Verlag GmbH
http://www.grin.com
Druck und Bindung: Books on Demand GmbH, Norderstedt Germany
ISBN 978-3-656-33130-8

ABSTRACT

This report addresses the reality of Wireless LAN security and performance. It provides an overview of security mechanisms and explains how security works in Wireless LAN networks. An in depth analysis of the Wired Equivalent Privacy (WEP), Wi-Fi protected access (WPA) and WPA2 standards is presented. The security vulnerabilities that exist in them are analyzed and explained. An experiment involving four devices (Dlink, Linksys, nanostationloco2 and a WBS) was done at Kampala international university. It was discovered from literature that most people prefer using WEP yet it is least secure. One study says 30% of all WLANs detected during network discovery experiment operate with WEP encryption. The study further proved that WEP can be compromised with 100% success. It was also discovered during the experiment that factors such as line of sight, obstruction, distance, antenna type, channel being used all affect network performance. The findings of this experiment can be used as guideline choosing the right encryption method and in designing a WLAN.

CHAPTER ONE

INTRODUCTION

Background

A decade ago hardly anyone heard of wireless networks but today, the IT technology is mostly based on the wireless connection followed by the development of wireless network-enabled devices (Cache and Liu, 2010). The manufacturers of the speed network equipment generate billions of pounds, yet a worldwide usage carries a number of risks costing their business overwhelming amounts of money and resources.

In Wireless Local Area Networks (WLAN) major issues are associated with security and at times performance problems arising from network overloads due to the ease with which people can connect to a given network. The wireless signal of the WLAN is broadcast through the air in all directions simultaneously. An unauthorized user can easily capture this signal using either a laptop or a freeware tools to exploit WLAN vulnerability. WLANs are increasingly used within home and business environment due to the convenience, mobility, and affordable prices for wireless devices. WLAN gives mobility and flexibility to users in homes and hot spot environments, such as airports and campuses. The wide range of usage emphasizes the importance of having a secure network and protection from potential break-ins.

According to Timothy and Linda(2004), encryptions such as WEP and WPA/WPA2 are used and this allows the transmitted data within the network to be encrypted but this does not guarantee total security because hacking specialists can access it (Cache and Liu, 2010).

Therefore, the main focus of this study will be to examine different encryption methods and to identify potential risks when using wireless networks and recommend possible means of securing WLANs.

Statement of the problem

Wireless LAN networks are generally designed with emphasis on convenience rather than security this is common in places where management would like to reach out to a much wider coverage than the sister wired network can go. This is exactly where the problem lies because, almost anyone with a WLAN enabled device can easily connect to and penetrate other users' systems in addition to increasing the amount of traffic on the network. Kampala international university experienced the same problem in 2011 after it acquire a WBS with a 5km radius coverage that so the whole of Gongo la mboto gain access to its " kiu wireless" network. This did not happen because no security measures had been taken but the security measures that had been implemented were weak and easy to compromise. As a result, the network broke a record of not being in position of opening even a single web page leading to a denial of service situation.

Objectives of the study

Main objective

The objective of this study was to evaluate WLAN encryption mechanisms and factors that affect WLAN performance

Specific Objectives

To examine the current wireless LAN security issues.

To identify factors that affect WLAN performance.

To make recommendations on how WLAN security and performance can be improved.

Research questions

Examine the current trend in WLAN security?

Which factors affect WLAN performance?

How can WLAN security and performance be improved?

Scope of the study

The study was carried out at KIU located in Gongo la mboto which is found in Ilala district, Dar es Salaam region.

The study involved literature analysis of three encryption mechanisms and several experiments aimed at evaluating different association time and factors that affect WLAN performance.

The encryption mechanisms were evaluated basing on literature and measurement of association time. Whereas performance was evaluated by measuring signal strength (number of network bars) and download speeds at different locations. The experiments involved four WLAN devices.

Significance of the study

The study findings can be used as a guideline for computer professionals on deciding which security mechanism to apply when they are working in different environments.

The study findings have expanded on the knowledge in the field of wireless networks performance and security.

The study findings have exposed major factors that affect WLAN performance

CHAPTER TWO

LITERATURE REVIEW

In this chapter, popular WLAN technologies and problems relevant to the research area are introduced. The aim is to provide an overview of wireless LAN securities and to evaluate the WLAN security issues.

Wireless LAN Security

There are currently three main encryption technologies available to WLAN communication; WEP, WPA, and WPA2. These technologies attempt to provide Confidentiality, Integrity and Authentication. However, they do not all succeed at these tasks and introduce vulnerabilities into the WLANs.

In the book written by Fluhrer, Martin and Shamir (2001), the first protection method and the easiest to use on wireless networks is Wired Equivalent Privacy (WEP). Although it appeared a successful invention, it could not survive for long and after only a period of two years, its RC4 was broken and this gave a bad reputation to wireless technology because of its perceived security flaw (Howard and Prince, 2010). The perceived flaws in the WEP saw the introduction of Wi-Fi Protected Access which is practically more efficient compared to WEP because it is much more complicated algorithm. As time went by, an improvement of WPA was made and that saw the introduction of WPA2.

WEP - Wired Equivalent Privacy

As the name suggests, according to Howard and Prince (2010), the objective of WEP designers, was never to make WLAN a 100 per cent secure, but to provide the same security as in a wired network. WEP was built for the encryption of the network traffic, the data integrity and station authentication. And despite its weaknesses, WEP is still widely deployed especially in organizations where security of information

is not a very big concern like in schools to allow students to easily connect to university's hot spots.

According to Beaver and McClure (2010), WEP uses a process of authentication to verify that a valid user is trying to connect to the network. In WEP there are two approaches to do this: open system authentication and shared key authentication. With Open Authentication, when a station wants to connect, the Access point always accepts the request and allows a station to join the network automatically. It uses a device-based authentication scheme as the user does not need to provide a valid user ID or password. Instead, the MAC address of the connecting node is used to identify it. Borisov (2001) in his early research highlights the possibility to configure the MAC addresses of the permitted clients with their access points. However, this approach does not provide the desired security as it is easy to spoof an address.

With Shared key Authentication, when a station requests for a connection, the AP sends a challenge-text in the form of a 40 or 128-bit number. The Station encrypts this text with the WEP secret key, sends it back to the AP which decrypts the text, checks if it is the correct one and then grants access to the network. This process only authenticates the station to the access point, not the other way around; therefore a malicious AP can simply pretend that the authentication was successful without knowing the secret key (Gast, 2005).

WEP uses the RC4 algorithm to encrypt data messages. This algorithm uses a stream cipher meaning that every byte is encrypted individually with the WEP key. The decryption is the reverse of this process and uses the same key (Fluhrer et al, 2001). Usually the cipher key has 128 bit and consist of 24 bit initialization vector (IV and 104 bit key). An IV is used to produce a single key-stream for each frame transmitted. The unique key is sent in plain text with the packet, therefore can be viewed by a packet sniffer (Lockhart, 2006). This is a major flaw of WEP encryption. As said by Flickenger (2006) the fact that the same key is used for all frames transmitted in the WLAN network it makes penetration test much easier.

WEP still provides basic security and it is integrated in most of the routers. In a survey conducted in all IT shops in Tanzania, it was discovered that all wireless devices they had on market supported this type of encryption and it is also supported by most laptops on the market.

According to Alikira, a network administrator KIU, WEP is easy to configure and also provides an option that does not require the client to even login and it is supported by most wireless devices and routers unlike WPA and WPA2 which are new and therefore not supported by some old laptops(interview,2012).

Walker (2000) concurs with other researchers that WEP is an unsafe encryption method and does not even meet its design goal which was to provide data privacy to the level of a wired network. Borisov et al (2001) presented the first serious paper on WEP insecurity receiving a high volume of controversy in the press. He would later be supported by Gast in 2005 who in his book published the same argued that, it only took a week for his group of students to crack the WEP key. An improved version of WEP called WEP+ was introduced later with patches by Agere systems. It greatly reduced the amount of weakness produced by normal WEP implementations and was released as a firmware update for their own access points (Burns, 2007). Cisco did not sit back it introduced the concept of Dynamic WEP Keys to their Aironet and Linksys WLAN Products and this also improved the WEP security. Unfortunately, all the above improvements were vendor specific which resulted in another limitation of incompatibility. In 2007, a new generation of WEP attacks was published by Tews, Weinmann, and Pyshkin. Their attack called PTW introduced new concepts, which allow breaking into WEP in less than a minute. The KoreK and PTW attacks were quickly integrated into WEP cracking and WLAN auditing tools and are now the standard for attacking WEP protected WLANs (Aircrack-ng, 2010).

WPA/WPA2 - Wi-Fi Protected Access

The design of WPA is based on a Draft 3 of IEEE 802.11i standard. It was proposed to ensure the release of a higher volume of security WLAN products before IEEE group could officially introduce 802.11i. Yet, major weaknesses of the WEP had

already been known at the time (IEEE-SA Standards Board, 2004). Due to those weaknesses, WPA introduced some improvements. First, WPA can be used with an IEEE 802.1x authentication server, where each user is given different keys and it can also be used in a less secure "pre-shared key" (PSK) mode, where every client is given the same pass-phrase just like with WEP (Lockhart, 2006).

In 2004, WPA2 standard was released to replace the less secure WEP and WPA. The final IEEE 802.11i standard not only adapts all the improvements included in WPA, but also introduces a new AES-based algorithm considered as fully secure (CPP UK, 2010).

WPA/WPA2 brings with it an improved level of security in WLANs can be implemented using WPA as in WEP. However, it does not include most of the flaws of the previous systems. The work on the WPA started immediately after the first reports of violation of the WEP and later on was deployed worldwide (Lowe, 2010). WPA includes two types of user authentication. One named WPA Personal with a pre-shared key mechanism similar to that of WEP and the WPA Enterprise, which uses 802.1X and derives its keys automatically (Lockhart, 2006). Nonetheless, the main improvement of the WPA was introduction of Temporal Key Integrity Protocol (TKIP) Instead of using a preshared key, which creates a key stream. It uses a pre-shared key to serve as the seed for generating the encryption keys (Lammle, 2010). WPA also uses the RC4 stream cipher with a 128-bit key and a 48bit IV, which is similar to the WEP for data encryption. However, unlike the WEP, there is a major improvement for WPA to use the Temporal Key Integrity Protocol (TKIP), which is the heart of WPA.

With a similar encryption process to WEP, implementation of the WPA is as simple as upgrading clients' software and updating the firmware of older access points (Lowe, 2010).

Like WPA, WPA2 offers two security modes: pre-shared key authentication based on a shared secret and authentication by an authentication server. Pre-shared key

authentication is intended for personal and small office use where an authentication server is unavailable (interview-data Alikira, 2012).

Like WPA, WPA2 networks use a pre-shared key and are vulnerable to the dictionary attacks (Phifer, 2007). Lockhart (2006) advises that, it is important to make the secret passphrase as long and as casual as possible (at least 20 characters long) with a mix of various random characters i.e. numbers, uppercases etc. WPA2 also introduces the authentication of Robust Security Network (RSN). "The RSN enhances the weak security of WEP and provides better protection for the wireless link by allowing the creation of Robust Security Network Associations (RSNA) only" (Cache and Liu, 2010).

In the article "Don't use WEP for Wi-Fi security" Sayer (2007) measures WPA encryption as a WEP replacement which is more secure and robust to attacks, yet it is able to run on the same hardware than WEP does. Nevertheless, the WPA shared more of the flaws of the WEP for example, in his book McMillan (2009) concluded that Pre-Shared Keying (PSK) is not secure and short and/or unsecure passwords are almost as disadvantageous as the WEP is. Based on similar thesis Takahashi (2004) developed a tool called WPAcrack, a proof of concept which allows a brute force offline dictionary attack against the WPA. He further concluded that the recommendation of the Wi-Fi alliance to use passwords longer than twenty characters would most likely not be executed in practice by the users of the WPA. Unfortunately, many people do not pay much attention to establishing long passwords and the consequences it may have in the future.

In 2008 security researchers Beck and Tews (2008) announced that they had developed a "systematic way to partially crack the Wi-Fi Protected Access 2". Before this attack, the only other known methods involved a dictionary attack against a weakly chosen pre-shared key. However, the new attack method poses a small threat to WPA2 overall as it does not work against AES the recommended encryption method for Enterprise Wireless LAN deployments by IEEE and Wi-Fi Alliance (McMillan, 2009).

The WPA/WPA2 are also subject to vulnerabilities affecting other 802.11i standard mechanisms such as attacks with 802.1X message spoofing and using the WPA2 protocol does not guarantee protection against attacks such as: frequency jamming, Denial of Service or de-authentication and de-association attacks. Though the improvements on WPA and WPA2 successfully provide more secure WLAN and make breaking into the network tougher. There are of course issues with TKIP (similarly to WEP) that allow small packets like ARP to be decrypted, yet there is no way to completely compromise a secure WPA key as well as it can be done with the WEP.

If the WPA is appropriately implemented and sufficiently managed, it will be a very strong security and highly difficult task of breaking; especially with the implementation of the AES-CCMP, which is the most secure wireless network configuration in use today (Alikira-interview,2012).

MAC Filtering

Every network card is identified by its unique MAC address. Although WLAN standard does not define Access Control, every AP nowadays implements MAC address filtering, often illustrated in the form of a simple list (Alikira, 2012). He goes on to say "last year, it is MAC filtering that saved our network". This mechanism could provide Authenticity, however MAC addresses are not as fixed as they appear to be. In result the MAC addresses can be forged rather easily however, Lockhart (2006) adds that, an attacker can without difficulty sniff the network traffic to see which stations are communicating in the network and can go ahead to forge or clone his Mac address.

Factor that affect wireless LAN performance

Current WLAN technologies (802.11B & G) provide great performance in the home environment, with few users and low traffic levels. The more limiting factor of the WLAN performance is broadband Internet link itself in play. These technologies are also being used in the corporate environment for some time and life has not proved so simple there, where demands are far more Onerous. The obvious factors include;

Distance from the Access Point; The further away you get from an AP, the more the signal strength drops and as the signal reduces the performance also degrades.

Physical obstacles; the 2.4 GHz is not good at penetrating solids. This has both bad and good effects. In a building sub-divided into rooms you can cover only a fairly small number of rooms with a single AP meaning you need more APs to cover, for instance, an entire school. On the other hand, the walls help form boundaries to allow APs on the same channel to co-exist in relative proximity to each other without interference.

Interference from other Wireless LANs; This is becomingly increasingly common in built-up city areas. In major cities it is not uncommon to be able to see in excess of twenty Wireless LANs from a single spot. It pays in designing and running your network to understand other businesses around you and work with them to avoid interference, to mutual benefit. Wireless Interference at 2.4 GHz is common, either from transient background sources or by other technologies which share unlicensed band – Bluetooth, some cordless Phones etc. Even to such things as faulty microwave ovens.

Coverage is always dictated by environment; In particular the materials and thickness of walls – especially if there is metal involved. Wire mesh is, for instance, a significant barrier to WLAN. For this reason a full Site Survey is still the most accurate way of assessing coverage needs. This involves actually trying it and seeing real results.

Network Load; the amount of data being transferred over the network can also greatly affect the performance of both wired and WLAN.

Incorrectly oriented antennas; All commonly deployed antennas have a degree of directionality; in the case of an Omni, for instance, the doughnut radiates at right angles to the stick of the antenna. It's critical to know this orientation, particularly when using APs with built-in antennas where it may not be obvious. It's a particular waste to physically mount an AP so virtually all of it's power is lost into the floor or ceiling!

Limited spectrum; Current areas of the radio spectrum available for WLAN have relatively limited "space". In particular, in the popular 2.4 GHz band used by 802.11B and G the 13 channels (11 in the US) a maximum of three Access Points can be deployed in the same coverage area. It's often not understood that, on a given channel, an 11b/g device spreads its transmission, to a significant degree, on the two channels directly above and the two channels directly below the central frequency. Therefore there should always be 5 channels between APs sharing airspace. In a single space, therefore, you'd usually find three APs configured for channels 1, 6 and 11. Note; channels 12 & 13 can't be used in the US; for this reason some WLAN clients don't support them at all.

Difficulties in limiting signal propagation; Particularly in open plan office areas it's difficult to control exactly how far a WLAN signal travels. This can limit the benefit from deploying multiple accesses into such an area. This can be managed to some degree with semi-directional antennas and manipulating radio power settings, but these have knock-on effects themselves.S

Multi-path fade; In complex environments multi-path fade (basically interference caused by signal reflections) causes significant loss in signal quality (note this is not a loss of strength). This can be overcome by using diversity antennas – two antennas placed the right distance apart on an AP. This distance largely ensures that, if signal quality is poor when communicating with a client via one of the antennas, the path via the alternate antenna will be free from multi-path fade.

Antenna polarization; WLAN is transmitted with the signal oriented in a specific your clients should be as closely aligned with this as possible to maintain maximum performance. This factor particularly affects point-to-point Wireless Bridge links.

Inflexible use of Antennas ;The standard antennas employed by most clients and Access Points, as they aim to provide a uniform transmission (a "doughnut" shape) in the horizontal plane and a relatively broad signal also in the vertical dimension, usually have a relatively low gain (transmission strength) – 2 bBi is common. High gain antennas are available which "focus" an APs radio power into a particular coverage pattern. This increases coverage in those areas at the expense of others.

Such antennas can also enhance security, for instance by reducing or eliminating coverage outside a building.

Securing a wireless network

Wireless LANs can bring incredible productivity and new efficiencies to organizations of all sizes. Properly deployed, WLANs can be as secure as wired networks. Use the following five steps as part of your deployment:

Create a WLAN Security Policy; a written wireless policy that covers authorized use and security is a necessary first step. Typically, security policy documents include the following sections: Purpose, Scope, and Policy, Responsibilities, Enforcement, definitions, and Revision history.

Secure the WLAN; securing the network should be based on three pillars: secure communications, threat control and containment, and policy and compliance management. With these areas in mind, following are best practices for securing your wireless network:

Secure Communications; Encrypt data and authenticate users of the network.

Modify the Default SSID; Change this default network naming immediately upon installation to something not directly related to your company. By default, access points broadcast the SSID to any wireless client within range. Disable the broadcast to reject people who may be casually looking for an open wireless network.

Use Strong Encryption; Configure a method of over-the-air security immediately after deployment. Use the most secure over-the-air encryption, which is either IEEE 802.11i or a VPN with mutual authentication between the network and the client.

Segment Users to Appropriate Resources; With identity networking, wireless devices need to authenticate only once with a WLAN system. Context information follows the devices as they roam, helping to ensure transparent mobility.

Ensure Management Ports Are Secured; The management interfaces of the WLAN system should support secure, authenticated methods of management. For

example, management should not be possible over the air and you should configure a separate management VLAN such that only specific stations have access to modify the WLAN network settings.

Protect Access Points; Cisco lightweight access points do not store encryption or other security information locally, so the network cannot be compromised if an access point is stolen. Prevent tampering by securing access points with a physical lock or deploying access points above a suspended ceiling.

Monitor the Exterior Building and Site; Because access point signals extend beyond the perimeter of most buildings, use management tools to prevent RF coverage from extending beyond the building perimeter. Make sure security personnel are aware of vehicles or people that seem to be loitering near the facility for extended periods of time.

Secure the Wireline Network against Wireless Threats; To prevent wireless intrusion, for example if you identify rogue devices on the network, you need to physically remove the rogue device to ensure that the wireless threat is permanently removed. The Cisco Wireless Location Appliance with Cisco WCS can precisely track up to 1500 Wi-Fi-enabled devices such as radio frequency identification (RFID) tags, Wi-Fi phones, laptops, and personal digital assistants.

Defend Against External Threats; The network must be protected from security threats, such as viruses, worms, and spyware, while mobile devices are away from the office. A compliance program needs to include monitoring to know when system and network policies are violated. Laptops need the same protections as the company network. Tools such as Cisco Security Agent consolidate endpoint security functions such as firewall, intrusion prevention, and spyware and adware protection in a single agent. User authentication through passwords, USB tokens, or smart cards can significantly strengthen security measures. For example, Cisco Network Admission Control (NAC) uses the network infrastructure to enforce security policy compliance on all devices seeking to access network computing resources.

Enlist Employees in Safeguarding the Company Network; Employee education, including informational posters and security best practices training (such as password selection and privacy), has proven effective in helping companies keep their confidential information and networks secure. With this in place, you can be at least to a small extent sure that your network will be secured.

CHAPTER THREE

METHODOLOGY

Research design

A descriptive longitudinal and experimental research design was used in the project. It is longitudinal because it was carried out at different places and times (day and night) and the experimental because it involved controlling, testing and measuring various variables. Four different wireless devices from three different manufacturers i.e. dlink, Linksys, wavion were used in the experiments. The aim was to practically measure their performance under different conditions and different levels of obstruction. The experiments were carried out in a simulated environment. Kiu computer block was used to simulate various environments for testing the Linksys and dlink integrated routers where as the KIU compound was used for evaluating the performance of the wavion base station and nanostationLoco2 both from unibiquiti. The computer block was chosen because of the many rooms that it has and it helped the researchers to test the effect of obstacles on the performance of indoor wireless devices.

Study Population

The experiment was carried by Mr. Alikira Richard .The experiments were carried out on two indoor network devices and two outdoor network devices namely; Dlink, Linksys, nanostationloco2 and WBS (wavion base station). The devices were selected because they were readily available at Kampala international university and also bearing in mind that the two brands are readily available and used in east Africa.

Research instrument

Observation method was used. Major the interest was placed on observing signal strength, download speed, and the ease with which both authorized and unauthorized users connect to the different devices.

Setup of the experiment

Requirements

1) 2 laptops with the same properties.

2) 1 kiu backup server

3) 1 Linksys router

4) 1 dlink router

5) 1 nanostationloco2 configured in routing mode

6) 1 WBS devices

7) 2 Data files with the same capacity (1GB each)

8) 2 straight through cables

Data collection procedure

The routers were all stationed in the server room of kiu and the laptops moved from one room to another by two people Starting from the server room, then the opposite offices, lab1 and the opposite room until lab four and the last room have been reached respectively. Remember, the two people will move at the same time but in opposite directions. Before moving from one room to another, the network connections will be disconnected first. After getting into the room, the people with laptops will have to reconnect their laptops and record the amount of time in seconds that it takes to connect to each of the indoor devices, the number of bars signifying the signal strength, time it takes to copy a 1 GB file from the server to the laptop. This will be done three times that is when the devices are configured using WEP, WAP, WAP2 and when Mac filtering is enabled with no authentication.

To test the effect of users on the network, the above procedure will repeated with only one laptop and the changes in both signal strength and download speed will be recorded.

Data analysis

The data collected will be entered into tables and frequencies and means calculated. The means from the indoor devices will be compared to ascertain the more efficient router of the dlink and Linksys. The same will be done for the outdoor devices to determine which of the two devices goes far away and can penetrate obstacles the more. This will be

Performance will be measured basing on the amount of time it takes to down load a 1 GB file at a 1m, 100m, 200m, 300m, 400m, 500,600m, 700m,800m,900m,1000m

3.7 Limitations

The only factor that may affect the outcome is that the simulated environment may not be exactly similar to what happens in the real world. Besides that, different walls are made out of different materials and therefore with different permeability levels.

With the outdoor devices, one of them uses an Omni antenna while the other uses a unidirectional antenna and this can be interpreted to mean that the two devices have different capabilities. In addition, based on the specification of the outdoor devices, the can go as far as five and more kilometers but the researcher will not be in position of going all that far.

It is also unclear whether these devices perform better when place at a high altitude or lower one and this might also interfere with the results.

CHAPTER FOUR

DATA PRESENTATION AND ANALYSIS

Objective one: To examine the current wireless LAN security issues

Research has it that security is perhaps the most important issue that should be addressed especially when dealing with data on organization's information system. From informal interviews with several networking practioners, it was discovered that there are four major ways of securing a WLAN these include WEP, WAP, WAP2 and MAC. These differ in their level of efficiency and the technologies that support them. WEP is support by older WLAN devices but some latest ones may not support it. It is the least efficient of all. WAP and WAP2 use a much more complicated algorithm that makes them more secure. WAP2 goes ahead and uses an encryption mechanism that even makes it more secure compared to WAP. This concurs with the views of (Fluhrer, Martin and Shamir, 2001). MAC filtering can be implemented in combination with either of the three mechanisms. It uses if-else conditions whereby if a device's Mac address is not on the list it is not allowed to associate itself.

Objective two: To identify factors that affect WLAN performance

Based of literature several factors were identified by different researchers and ; coverage, speed, obstruction were tested.

Table 4.1: showing Signal strength of indoor devices

location	Connected to Dlink	Connected to Linksys
Server room	5	5
HOD	5	5
Lab1	5	5
Lab2	4	3
Lab3	3	2
Lab4	2	2
End of block	2	1

Figure 4.1: showing signal strength

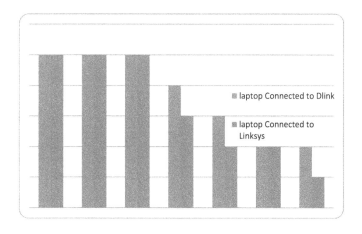

From the graph, it can be observed that as the distance increases the signal strength reduces. The increase in the number of obstacles (walls) also affects signal strength and that is why the number of bars go on reducing as you move from the serve room to the extreme end of the building.

Table 4.2: showing download Speed in seconds both on channel six

Laptop	Connected to Dlink	Connected to Linksys
Server room	340	265
HOD	330	304
Lab1	401	297
Lab2	474	430
Lab3	643	667
Lab4	638	607
End of building	814	720

Figure 4.2: showing the effect of distance and obstacles on download speed

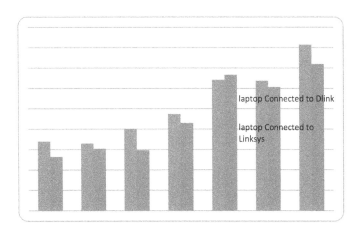

While in the server room, it take 264 and 340 seconds for laptops connected to Linksys and dlink wireless routers respectively to download 1 GB of data from a server wired to each of the two routers . As the distance and number of obstacles increase, there is a steady increase of time taken to download the same amount of data. The increase in time required signifies the decrease in speed.

Table 4.3: showing Download Speed in seconds with devices on different channels

Location of laptop	Dlink on channel 11	Linksys on channel 1
Server room	280	190
HOD	290	180
Lab1	330	285
Lab 2	370	341
Lab3	420	320
Lab4	404	462
End of block	480	532

Figure 4.3: showing Download Speed in seconds with devices on different channels

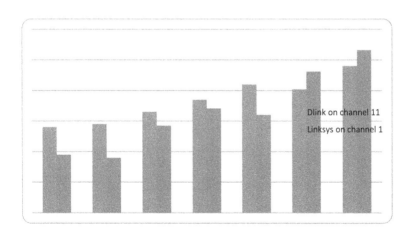

While in the server room, it take 190 and 280 seconds for laptops connected to Linksys using channel 1 and dlink using channel 11 wireless routers respectively to download 1 GB of data from a server wired to the each of the two routers. As the distance and number of obstacles increase, there is a steady increase of time taken to download the same amount of data. The increase in time required signifies the decrease in speed (performance). Comparing figure 4.3 with figure 4.2, in figure 4.3 the time has slightly lowered which is a sign that the download speeds are higher yet the amount of data, computers, and routers has not changed. Which means the difference (increase in performance) must be as a result of each router using a separate channel.

Table 4.4: Dlink's performance comparison

Location of laptop	separate channel	shared channel
Server room	280	340
HOD	290	330
4	330	401
3	370	474
Lab3	420	643
Lab4	404	638
End of block	480	814

Figure 4.4: showing comparison of dlink download performance

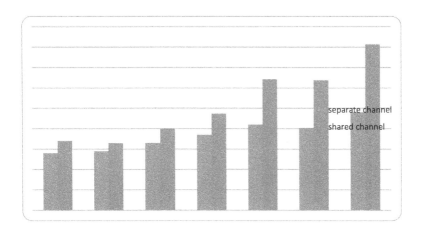

It is evident from the graph that it takes less time to download a file from a server when the devices are not sharing a channel with another device that when the channel is shared. The less time reciprocates to mean better performance.

Table 4.5: showing Linksys' performance comparison

Location of laptop	On separate channels	On a shared channel
Server room	190	265
HOD	180	304
Lab1	285	297
Lab 2	341	430
Lab3	320	667
Lab4	462	607
End of block	532	720

Figure 4.5: showing Linksys' performance comparison

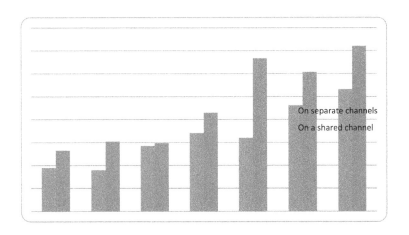

It is evident from the graph that it takes less time to download a file from a server when the devices are not sharing a channel with another device that when the channel is shared. The less time reciprocates to mean better performance.

Table 4.6: showing Association time

encryption	WEP		WAP		WAP2		MAC	
location	*Dlink*	*Linksys*	*Dlink*	*Linksys*	*Dlink*	*Linksys*	*Dlink*	*Linksys*
Server room	3	4	2	4	3	5	2	4
HOD	5	5	3	5	5	5	2	4
Lab1	3	5	4	5	4	6	3	5
Lab2	5	15	6	14	6	5	5	4
Lab3	6	8	6	13	7	6	5	5
Lab4	6	12	5	14	5	13	6	7
End of block	8	10	9	11	7	10	7	9

Figure 4.6: showing association time when using

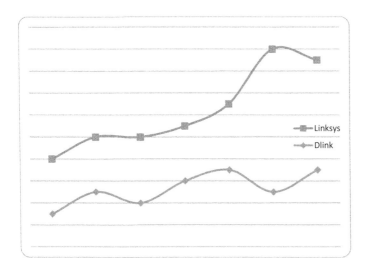

Figure 4.7: showing association time when using WAP

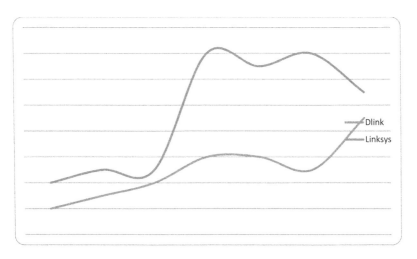

Figure 4.8: showing association time when using WAP2

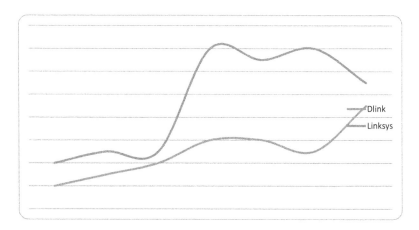

Figure 4.9: showing association time MAC filtering is enabled

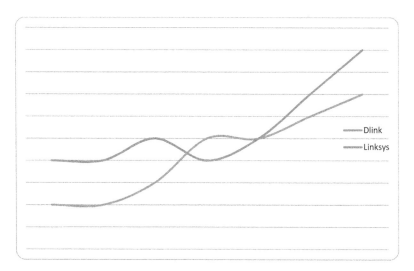

Table 4.7 showing Outdoor devices observational form

Room	Signal Strengt *Nanotationloc*	*Wavion*	Downlo ad *Nanotationloc*	Speed in *wavion*	Connection Speed with WE P *Nanotationloc*	*wavion*	W AP *Nanotationloc*	*wavion*	W AP *Nanotationloc*	*wavion*	MA C *Nanotationloc*	*wavion*
admissions	4	5	320	213	4	9	5	9	4	8	6	8
administration	1	5	523	304	5	7	6	8	5	7	5	7
Law department	2	3	257	276	4	8	6	10	7	10	5	9
Staff quarters	0	4	##	340	##	9	##	9	6	8	##	8
At canteen	1	3	##	488	##	8	##	8	8	9	##	8
At gongolamb oto	0	1	##	##	##	##	##	##	#	#	#	#
At computer block	5	5	206	270	4	7	8	9	7	8	6	9

Table 4.8 showing Signal strength of outdoor devices

Location of laptop	Nanostationloco2	wavion
Admissions	4	5
Administration	1	5
Law department	2	3
Staff quarters	0	4
At canteen	1	3
At gongolamboto	0	1
At computer block	5	5

Figure 4.10: showing the effect of distance on download speed

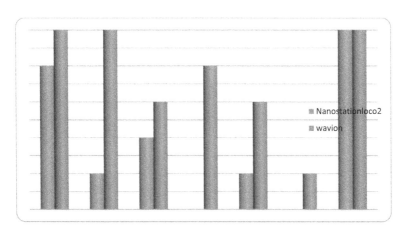

With knowledge of the different locations on the graph, it is clear that the far away the location of the laptop, the weaker the signal. That is why for example at Gongo lamboto which happens to be the farthest, wavion device had one bar while the nanostationloco2 device had none. In comparison with the computer block where both devices are located, both devices had all the five bars present which means distance affects the signal strength of wireless devices.

Table 4.9: showing the influence of distance on download speed

Location of the laptop used	Download speed in seconds	
	Nanotationloc2	*wavion*
Admissions	320	213
Administration	523	304
Law department	257	276
Staff quarters	##	340
At canteen	##	488
At gongolamboto	##	##
At computer block	206	270

A comparison of download speed for two outdoor devices shows the closer to the devices the laptop was from the devices the less the time was required to download 1 GB of data. However, as the distance increased, the speed dropped and the time that was required increased. Some places with (##) could not download or even connect at all because either there was no signal at all or the signal was present but too weak to establish a connection.

Figure 4.11: showing the influence of distance on download speed

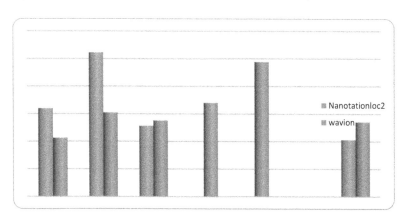

Table 4.10: showing time taken for a laptop to associate with outdoor devices

Location of laptop	Association speed							
	WEP		WAP		WAP2		MAC	
	Nanotationloc2	*wavion*	*Nanotationloc2*	*wavion*	*Nanotationloc2*	*wavion*	*Nanotationloc2*	*Wavion*
Admissions office	4	9	5	9	4	8	6	8
Administration	5	7	6	8	5	7	5	7
Law department	4	8	6	10	7	10	5	9
Staff quarters	#	9	#	9	6	8	#	8
At canteen	#	8	#	8	8	9	#	8
At gongolamboto	#	#	#	#	#	#	#	#
At computer block	4	7	8	9	7	8	6	9

By observation, a WBS requires more time to associate with a laptop than a nanostationloco2 device. Furthermore, as the distance increases the association times slightly changes by a factor of 1-2 seconds which means association time is not so much affected by distance as long as the device's network is within reach. The high time taken by WBS could be due to the fact that WBS is Omni direction and therefore uses more energy than its counterpart nanostationloco2 which is unidirectional.

CHAPTER FIVE

FINDINGS, CONCLUSIONS AND RECOMMENDATIONS

Finding on performance

a)   It was discovered that, when the operating system notifies you about a weak Wi-Fi signal, it probably means that your connection is not as fast and as reliable as it could be. Worse, you might lose your connection entirely in some parts of your networks coverage. This was reached after observing the changes in signal strength and download speeds. It was observed that as the number of bars (signal strength) reduced, the download time proportionally increased with a respective degradation in performance.

b)   It was also discovered that, signals strength reduces with the increase in distance from the AP and also with the number of obstacles in the line of site. Looking at figure4.4, as the laptops were moved from the server room, to HOD's office, lab1, then to lab2, then to lab3 and so on, the number of bars kept on reducing implying a decrease in signal strength which can be interpreted as decrease in performance.

c)   To confirm that, download speed was also measured i.e. from the server room, to HOD's office, lab1, then to lab2, then to lab3, till the end of building and the download speed kept on increasing which was confirmatory for the decrease in the two devices performance. Not all the devices indoor and outdoor relatively behaved similarly in both signal strength and download speed.

Conclusion on performance

Based on the findings, performance of WLANs in affected by the following; distance from the AP, the obstacles in between the AP and the client, the channel interference, the strength of the device, the antennae, the type of the antennae (Omni and unidirectional), weather among others. Download speed will also depend on the distance, amount traffic on the network among others.

Also most wireless devices do not cover as much area as their manufacturers claim. This was evidenced when the WBS device failed to even go beyond one kilometer yet its manufacturers claim that it can go as far as five kilometers

The type of antennae being used also affects performance. For example an omnidirectional antenna requires a lot of power to propagate signals in multiple directions compared to single directional antennae that requires approximately a quarter of the power needed by the Omni. That is why, given the same amount of power, a unidirectional antenna can cover a much bigger area than an equivalent Omni antenna.

Recommendations on performance

Position your wireless router, modem router, or access point in a central location where all clients can easily connect to it. For example, if your router is on the first floor and your PC or laptop is on the second floor, place the router high on a shelf in the room where it is located.

The router should be away from walls and floors; Metal objects, walls, and floors will interfere with your router's wireless signals. The closer your router is to these obstructions, the more severe the interference, and the weaker your connection will be.

Use a unidirectional antenna; if your router's antenna is removable, you can upgrade to a high-gain antenna that focuses the wireless signals in only one direction. You can even aim the signal in the direction you need it most.

Always ensure that your PC's card is working properly. This is Wireless network signals must be sent both to and from your computer. Sometimes your router can broadcast strongly enough to reach your computer, but your computer can't send signals back to your router. To improve this, replace your laptop's PC card-based wireless network adapter with a USB wireless network adapter that uses an external antenna.

You can also use a wireless repeater to extend your wireless network range without requiring you to add any wiring. By placing the wireless repeater halfway between your wireless router or AP and your computer, you will boost your wireless signal strength.

Change your wireless channel; Wireless routers can broadcast on several different channels, similar to the way radio stations use different channels. Just as you will sometimes hear interference on one radio station while another is perfectly clear, sometimes one wireless channel is clearer than others. Changing your routers channel can improve on the performance.

Update your firmware and NIC drivers. This can improve performance. Similarly, network adapter vendors occasionally update the software that Windows uses to communicate with your network adapter, known as the driver.

Upgrade 802.11a, 802.11b, and 802.11g devices to 802.11n; Although wireless-G (802.11g) may be the most common type of wireless network, wireless-N (802.11n) is at least twice as fast and it has better range and stability. Wireless-N is backward-compatible with 802.11a, 802.11b, and 802.11g, so you can still use any existing wireless equipment that you have though you won't see much improvement in performance until you upgrade your computer or network adapter to wireless-G, too.

Findings on security

WLANs are changing the way people work. They provide high-speed Internet connections in public locations and in homes or work places. You can access them with a wireless-ready mobile PC, such as a laptop, notebook, Smartphone, or any

35

other mobile device equipped with a wireless card. These networks range from paid services, such as T-Mobile or Verizon Wireless, to free, public connections (hot spots). Hot spots are everywhere, including coffee shops, restaurants, libraries, bookstores, airports, trains, and hotel lobbies. Just like managed WLANs are in schools, hospitals and other organizations. Many of these places will inform you that they have a hot spot for wireless Internet use and will tell you how to access it, including providing you with a password, if necessary.

It was also discovered that, there are four major mechanisms provided by most WLAN devices and they include; WEP, WAP, WAP2 and MAC. WEP is older having been introduced in around 2001 and is supported by most computers but it's the weakest to hack of the four. WAP and WAP2 were introduced after discovering a lot of flaws in WEP. They use a much more complicated algorithm that makes them more secure compared to WEP. WAP2 goes uses an AES encryption mechanism that even makes it better than WEP and WAP. This concurs with the views of (Fluhrer, Martin and Shamir, 2001).

One respondent and network administrator at one of the leading institutions in Tanzania said that MAC filtering can be used to decide on who should access and who should. He adds this method is more effective because it can be used together with any of the; WEP, WAP and WAP2.

Conclusions on security

Wireless networks especially public hot spots are vulnerable to security breaches. That is why you should never simply try to connect to a wireless network with your PC or phone. Network professionals need to consider implementing strong security measures such as, data and password encryption, user authentication MAC and web filtering among others to ensure the safety of their clients.

According to Fluhrer, Martin and Shamir (2001),the three security types supported by most wireless devices compare in the following order; WAP2 is the most effective followed by WAP and then WEP. Each of these can be implemented together with

MAC filtering, firewalls, data encryptions among others to enhance the overall network security.

Recommendations on security

To WLAN users:

For networks that house very confidential information, should use a couple of security mechanisms. Of the three (WEP, WAP and WAP2), WAP2 seems to outperforms the other two. Its effectiveness is however improved when it is used together with Mac filtering, encryption, certificates among others. This done not mean that WEP and WAP should not be used. The whole issue lies in the fact that WEP and WAP algorithms can easily be hacked.

You should disable your Wi-Fi adapter whenever you are not using it. Otherwise your computer might connect to a malicious hot spot without you realizing it.

Try to choose more secure connections; for example those networks that require a network security key or have some other form of security, such as a certificate because the information sent over these networks is encrypted, and encryption can help protect your computer from unauthorized access.

You can use https for emails; Even if the email provider you use has a secure network, after you log on to your account on a public network, your information is no longer encrypted unless you use a more secure connection like https.

Always activate your firewall. This will protect your PC by preventing unauthorized users from gaining access to your computer through the Internet or a network. It acts as a barrier that checks all incoming information and then either blocks the information or allows it to come through.

Monitor your access points; Chances are that there are multiple wireless networks anywhere you are trying to connect. These connections are all access points, because they link into the wired system that gives you Internet access. Configure your PC to let you approve access points before you connect.

Disable file and printer sharing especially when you are using your computer on a public network. This is because, when it is enabled, it leaves your computer vulnerable to hackers.

Make your folders private to make them more difficult for hackers to access your files. You can protect your files further by encrypting them, which requires a password to open or modify them.

Do not keep sensitive data on your portable computer; Instead, save it on a corporate network share or on a password-protected site, such as Windows Live SkyDrive, and access it only when necessary.

Network professionals should put the security of their clients at the forefront. Using more efficient mechanisms like; WAP2, web filtering, encryption, Mac filtering to ensures that only authorized clients gain access to your network and this ensure good performance, system auditing and accountability in case of a security breach. Dynamic authentication has proved to be efficient since it requires the user to login every time a client wants to connect to your network.

Bibliography

Beaver, K. and McClure, S. (2006). Hacking For Dummies, (2nd Ed.)

Beaver, k. and Peter, T. D. (2005). Hacking Wireless Networks For Dummies by, Wiley Publishing, Inc.

Bruce, N. W. (2000). Hacking Wireless Networks For Dummies, Wiley Publishing, Inc.

http://www.northrup.org

Hurley, C. (2007). War Driving & Wireless Penetration Testing, Syngress Publishing, Inc.

Matthias, K. D. and Matt, W. (2005). Running Linux, (5th Ed.), O'Reilly Media, Inc.

www.aircrack-ng.org